COLOURS GUIDE

MUSEUMS

HOUSE OF THE KING

PANTHEONS

MONASTERY

BASILICA

LIBRARY

COLLEGE

MAIN FAÇADE

PALACE OF THE BOURBONS

GARDENS

Main floor

Ground floor

Basement

Real Monasterio de San Lorenzo de El Escorial

CARMEN GARCÍA-FRÍAS
JOSÉ LUIS SANCHO

REALES SITIOS DE ESPAÑA

© PATRIMONIO NACIONAL, 1999
Palacio Real de Madrid
Bailén, s/n
28071 Madrid
Tel. 91 547 53 50

© Texts: Carmen García-Frías and
José Luis Sancho Gaspar

© Photographs: Patrimonio Nacional - Félix Lorrio

NIPO: 006-99-026-X
ISBN: 84-7120-251-4
National book catalogue number: M–45471-1999

Coordination and production: ALDEASA
Translation: Word Works
Design and layout: Myriam López Consalvi
Photograph setting: Lucam
Printed: Estudios Gráficos Europeos, S. A.

Cover photograph: A view of the Monastery as seen from
Monte Abantos.

Back cover photograph: Monastery pastureland.

Printed in Spain

Contents

ATRIMONIO NACIONAL (National Heritage) is
e institution which manages those properties
 the State which are at the service of the
rown for performing representative functions
 commended by the Constitution and Laws
 Spain.

The institution manages a number of
laces, as well as several Monasteries and
onvents founded by Spanish monarchs, all of
 eat historical, artistic and cultural importance
 d, most significantly, of great *symbolic value*.
he Royal Palaces of Madrid,
 Pardo, Aranjuez, San Ildefonso and La
lmudaina are used as residential and
presentative buildings as was intended when
ey were built centuries ago and it is here
here His Majesty the King performs his
uties as Head of State, particularly in the
oyal Palace of Madrid, where this *symbolic
lue* is felt most strongly, as the official
sidence of the Crown.

In harmony with these functions, the other
uildings and properties which make up
atrimonio Nacional have a decidedly cultural
urpose and are places of study and research,
 well as being open to the general public.

Both the buildings and the Spanish royal
llections (27 in all, ranging from fans to tools
 nd which include silverware, paintings,
pestries, furniture, musical instruments,
ocks, etc.) are remarkable for a number of
haracteristics which go to make Patrimonio
Jacional a unique cultural institution: their
 rticular purpose, as they are still considered
alid for representative use by the Crown; their
istorical authenticity, as they are all pieces
 hich have been ordered, acquired or offered
 s gifts at some time for that particular place;

their *originality*, which can be seen by the
absence of replicas and imitations, and their
extraordinary artistic, historical and symbolic value.

The combination of such impressive
characteristics makes it clear to the visitor that
Patrimonio Nacional is much more than a
simple museum.

The Spanish Royal Palaces are surrounded
by approximately 20,500 hectares of open land.
Around 500 hectares are given over to gardens
or farmland, while the remaining 20,000
hectares are forest, divided between El Pardo,
La Herrería and Riofrío and part of which is
open to the general public. These woodlands,
mainly of the biotype *Mediterranean forest*, are
of renowned ecological importance, the value
of which is at a par with the monuments found
in their midst.

The Royal Monasteries and Convents have
been attended by the same religious orders
since their foundation, with the exception of
San Lorenzo de El Escorial, originally of the
Hieronymite Order, which was passed over to
the Augustinian Order following the sale of
Church lands in the 19th century. They enjoy
particular importance in the history of Spain, as
their origin dates back to the particular
patronage of the monarchs of the era.

By being open to the general public, not
only do these buildings fulfil a cultural
purpose, they allow the Spanish people to
capture their symbolic value, identify with it
and consider themselves a legatee of the vast
historical and artistic treasures which make up
the properties of Patrimonio Nacional.

Collected over the centuries by the Crown,
their influence in the cultural identity of Spain
has been, and still is, decisive.

Introduction

THE EL ESCORIAL Monastery is the monument which best represents the ideological and cultural aspirations of the Spanish Golden Age". During this era, the Spanish Crown, which was the leading world power not only for its dynastic alliances and resulting territorial power in Europe, but also for its control of over almost all of the recently discovered American continent, established itself as the main defender of the Catholic Counter-Reformation as opposed to those countries which had embraced the Protestant Reform.

The "Catholic King's struggle for European hegemony, the defense of the traditional religion, and the worship of dynasty and of the Monarch as one of God's chosen people, are strongly reflected in El Escorial by its original combination of Italian and Flemish artistic forms.

At the present time, El Escorial continues under the royal trust of H.M. the King and its management and tutelage is dealt with by the National Patrimony before starting out on our visit around the monument, it might be worthwhile taking a quick look at some historical details.

General comments

The reasons for the foundation

AN LORENZO el Real was originally designed for a variety of purposes: as a monastery for the monks of the order of St. Jerome, whose church was the pantheon of Emperor Charles V, and of his wife, his son, Philip II, his relatives and heirs, and where the monks prayed endlessly for the salvation of the royal family; as a palace to house the King, patron of the foundation, and his entourage; the college and seminary complete the religious function of the Monastery, while the Library complements these three focal points.

The victory over Henry II of France in *Saint Quentin,* the first conquest in Philip II's reign, coincided with San Lorenzo's Day on August 10th, 1557. This led, in part, to the naming of the Monastery, which is not simply a votive monument.

Charles V also played a part in the Monastery's foundation given the enormous influence he had over his son's spirit, which can be seen by Philip II's wish to give his father a dignified burial after Charles V had spent his last years among the Hieronymite monks of Yuste.

The founder

PHILIP II was King of Naples, Sicily and Milan from 1554, and King of the Netherlands a year later when a series of cessions were made by his father, Emperor Charles V, who retired to the Monastery of Yuste in 1556 and passed on the Crown of Spain and the New World to his son before he died in 1558.

The work

HAVING DECIDED to build the Monastery, Philip II began his search of the ideal site in 1558, which he finally located in 1562. Work began on the project or "universal design" drawn up by Juan Bautista de Toledo. By 1571, the Monastery area was almost complete; work commenced on the King's House in 1572 and on the Basilica in 1574, which was consecrated in 1595, the

Palace Garden.

year in which most agree the Monastery was completed. Nonetheless, although the last stone was placed in 1584, a few more years were spent on its decoration. The King personally supervised all of the construction, responsibility for which fell to the architect, the prior and two commissions.

The architect was directly named by the King. As such, he only answered to Philip II and not to the prior, who was considered the maximum authority by everone else and who headed the "Congregation", the executive commission in charge of judicial and financial affairs, inspections and payments.

The artisans

EL ESCORIAL can by no means be considered the work of single architect, but the product of close collaboration between two men: Juan Bautista de Toledo and Juan de Herrera. Juan Bautista de Toledo, who had worked under Michelangelo in the Vatican, was charged with drawing up plans for the main body of the Monastery and most of the designs. Juan de Herrera was responsible for the completion of the complex, including several parts of the buiding which had not been designed by Toledo. If one takes into account further contributions to the building by several other Spanish and Italian architects, then the final result of El Escorial must be seen as a very personal manifestation of Philip II's character.

Neither must one forget the contribution made by the master builders and the overseers, such as Brother Antonio de Villacastin, Pedro de Tolosa, Diego de Alcantara or Juan de Minjares. Francisco de Mora was a disciple of Herrera who continued this architect's work from 1583 onwards. In the 18th century, the spirit of El Escorial shaped the classically

General view of the Monastery from the Little House of the Prince.

Italian-trained Juan de Villanueva's work on the mejor projects he carried out on the Monastery for Charles III and Charles IV.

El Escorial from the 16th to the 19th centuries

THE INSTITUTION remained faithful to the desires and plans of its founder until 1835, and was enriched by the contributions made by the succeeding monarchs.

Philip III began work on the *Pantheon*. Philip IV completed it and enhanced its collection of paintings with some major works. Charles II had Bartolome Zumbigo rebuild the Monastery after it burned down in 1671, and redecorate it with a *retable* of the Sacristy and a series of grandiose *frescoes* by Luca Giordano. From 1767 onwards, Charles III ordered a residential area to be built in Real Sitio, with the new houses of "la Lonja" and the two *"little houses of pleasure"* for the Prince and his brother. Charles IV had the northern façade remodelled and the Palace of the Bourbons decorated as well as having the decoration of the *Casita*, which he had had built while he wa still Prince, enriched.

El Escorial in the 19th and 20th centuries

AFTER THE losses suffered by the El Escorial art collection during the War of Independence, partially compensated for by Fernando VII's returns and restorations, the disentailing laws (the 19th century obliged the community of Hieronymite monks to abandon the Monastery and led to the channelling of the foundation's wealth to the Patrimony of the Crown. The Monastery was then destined for use by different religions until the Augustinian monk appeared in 1885. The celebrations of the IV

▲ *Above, Monastery roofs. Below, Main Entrance to the Monastery.*

King's gardens from a balcony.

Centennial commemorating the beginning of the construction in 1963, and its completion in 1986, granted momentum to the works of restoration and to studies on El Escorial, which seem to have left behind those positive or negative evaluations that were so blinded by prejudice.

The visit

THE SAN LORENZO el Real Monastery of El Escorial consists of a huge rectangle within which the following areas designed for separate functions are distributed, as can be seen from the plan:

The sacred area of the Church and its atrium.
The Convent, laid out around one big and four small patios.
The House of the King.
The outbuildings of the Palace of the King.
The College.
The Library.

This "universal design" drawn up by Juan Bautista de Toledo is influenced by the cross-shaped floor plans of 15th century Italian and Spanish hospitals, but it is generally thought that its main inspiration comes from the traditional layout of medieval monasteries.

The Monastery is situated on the mountain side, orientated towards the four cardinal points, with the altar facing East in such a way that this and the South side, where the land slopes down, are enclosed by gardens supported by thick walls. The Northern and Western sides, where the land is higher, are surrounded by an area of deference called "la Lonja" (the Porch).

As the ascent comes to an end, the most picturesque aspect of the building comes into

REAL MONASTERIO DE SAN LORENZO DE EL ESCORIAL

View of the south facade of the Monastery, with the Convalescent Gallery and the orchard pond. ▲

◀ *On the previous page, general night view of the Monastery.*

sight, with the House of the King, the rear of the Basilica and its dome. You can only reach the main *Façade* by crossing "la Lonja" and encircling the whole building. The Monastery is impressive for its uniformity and lack of ornamentation, with each fac,ade conserving its own individual character.

Juan Bautista de Toledo did not originally plan for so much uniformity. He imagined the western part of the building with one floor less and towers in the centres of the northern and southern façades giving it much more height. The variation in the building's forms would have given it a harmonious style more in keeping with the late Renaissance. In 1564, Philip II decided to double the number of monks in the Monastery community to one hundred instead of fifty, and thus raised the whole building to four floors At the centre of the northern façade, the door gives on to the visitor's access, where the entrance ticket can be purchased. Having acquired one's ticket, it is a good idea to go out once again and go towards the main doorway, the northern façade and the buildings which surround La Lonja, constructed between the XVI and XVII centuries, are considered as being mere outbuildings of the Palace and Monastery.

The two *Workers'Houses* are situated opposite the northern façade. Remodelled in the 18th century by Juan de Villanueva, they were built by Juan de Herrera in the 16th century to lodge the King's servants, and later joined to the Palace in 1769 by an *underground passage*, built by Father Pontes (Friar Antonio de San José), to protect the royal attendants' wigs and three-cornered hats from the strong winds. *The Compaña* to the south-west of "la Lonja" and constructed at the end of the 16th century by Francisco de Mora for the monks'servants is joined to the Monastery by a gallery built on arches.

Up until Charles III's reign, there were no buildings of any significance around the Monastery: the main façade faced the mountain in an exchange of Nature and Art. The Hieronymite monks lived like hermits and dedicated their time to prayer in the midst of the wilderness.

The other buildings that close off "la Lonja", are therefore, the work of Juan de Villanueva in the 18th century. Next to the Compana, the *Houses* of *the Infantes* or King's children, begun in 1771 and, at an angle to this building, the *State Minister's House* both have splendid staircases.

The main façade of the Monastery has three porticos. The side porticos, identical in execution, correspond to the College (on the left) and the Convent (on the right).

The Convent's portico does not correspond to its main entrance, but to a ramp which leads on to the food stores and, behind them, to the huge *kitchen* and skylight-roofed patio situated between the for lesser cloisters. The layout is more or less similar to that of the College, which boasts an aula magna or "theatre".

The main portico, situated in the centre of this façade, leads onto the Monastery and Basilica and is therefore considered to be religiously emblematic in design. It does not, however, bear any relation to the building on which it leans, the library in this case, but rather to the church whose real façade is situated at the end of the atrium.

In fact, Herrera got the inspiration for this facade from an engraving by Serlio, and he was backed in his choice by Philip II himself who was no newcomer to the masteries of architecture. The royal coat-of-arms and the *St Lawrence* were created by Juan Bautista Monegro.

By crossing the vestibule, over which the Library lies, one gains access to the Patio of Kings, dominated by the large dome and the Basilica façade.

Basilica's Main Altarpiece. ▶

The sculpture of the six great kings of Judea and that of St. Lawrence, set on a single base, are again by Juan Bautista Monegro. All seven figures were sculptured from the same chunk of stone, from a quarry in the mountains, on which the following message was carved: "six kings and a saint / emerged from the rock / and there was still room for more." The Patio was originally designed by Juan Bautista de Toledo with side porticos, but these were never built. The righthand tower is the watchtower the lefthand equivalent was named "of the chimes" after a Flemish organ, restored and re-installed in 1988.

On ascending to the Basilica portico, we encounter a doorway in the wall on the right: it was the old main entrance to the Monastery, and it is through this doorway we will leave once we have completed our visit.

The Basilica

THIS GREAT monastic church is the true "raison d'être" of El Escorial. Although Juan Bautista de Toledo set the location and boundaries within his "universal design", they were not his alone which provided the end result, but rather a combined effort, to which Juan de Herrera added a variety of different influences and styles.

Juan Bautista de Toledo's designs included a semi-circular apse flanked by towers; the engineer-architect, Franceso Paciotto, strongly criticized its general proportions in 1562 and suggested in 1563 a square-shaped design. Toledo developed another project in 1567 and, from this year on until 1572, Philip II had the best Italian architects present their plans, which were examined, along with the Spanish projects, by the Florentine Academy and by Vignola in Rome. After studying all the plans in 1573, he decided they were not what he was

looking for and did not make his decision unt 1574. Philip II finally opted, apparently due to Herrera's influence, for Paciotto's project. The final result is similar to the Genovese church c Santa Maria of Carignano by G. Alessi. The organizing skills of Juan de Herrera and the overseer, Brother Antonio de Villacastin, excelled in the construction work.

The Basilica really consists of two churches the people's church, or the *Sotocoro*, and the Royal chapel and the monastic church which make up the main body.

The ground plan of the *Sotocoro* is a repeat, on a smaller scale, of the high church, whose central area is covered by a rather daring flat cupola. Two altars on each side of the central arch were used for giving mass to the town people. Between this area and the Royal Chape there is the *Seminarists' Choir* area, which is separated by large bronze railings cast by Tujarón in Saragossa.

On the same level as the main floor above the Sotocoro, you can find the *Monks' Choir* area which is closed to the public; the cabinet work on the chairs and the organ cases were by the Genovese, Jose Flecha. One of the 124 chairs located in the southwest corner is slightly wider than the others: it was used by Philip II to listen to the service in the Choir area. The fresco on the cupola, *The Glory*, was painted by Luca Cambiasso, known in Spain as Luqueto.

Several portraits are painted here, such as the one of the artist himself and the overseer, Villacastín. The paintings on the walls were completed by Romulo Cincinnato.

Before going through the bronze railings, your attention is drawn to the *High Chapel*, with its enormous high altarpiece at the back and the *royal cenotaphs* at the sides, according to a classic canonical design by Juan de Herrera. All the gilded bronze sculpture work is by the two Milanese artists, Leone and Pompeo Leoni.

Above left, general view of the Basilica from the high corridors, and on the right, view of the Basilica's vaults and dome. Below, the Choir. ▶

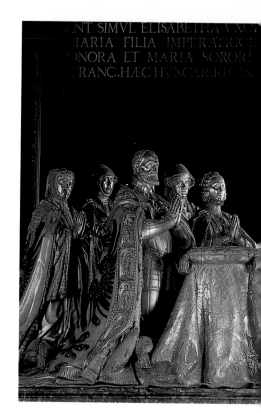

Worth noting further inside is the beautiful tiny chapel, the *Tabernacle*, designed by Herrera and built between 1579 and 1586 by Jacome Trezzo with a variety of different Spanish marbles. The two canvasses in the first level of the Basilica and the central canvass of the second are by Pellegrino Tibaldi. The rest are by Federico Zuccaro.

The cenotaphs, of Charles V on the Gospel side (left) and Philip II on the Epistle side (right), are crowned by their respective coat-of-arms. There are three doors situated below the cenotaphs: the nearest one leads from the pulpit to the Sacristy and the Reliquary, and the other two lead onto the small private chapels next to the King and Queen's bedroom.

This arrangement is a copy of the Emperor's quarters in Yuste. It is also meant thus, it may be said that Philip II practically

slept above his tomb, and prayed below the place appointed for his own burial statue. Philip II is surrounded by his wives: Isabella (Valois, María of Portugal (the mother of Princ Charles who is at her side) and Ana of Austria Opposite, next to an armed Charles V wearing the royal mantle, is the Empress Isabella (Philip II's mother); behind her, her daughter, Maria; and next, the Emperor's sisters, María (Hungary and Leonor of France.

The *ceiling of the Presbytery* is decorated, as is the Choir area, with frescoes by Luqueto an depict *The Coronation of the Virgin*. The remaining ceilings were coated with stucco in the 16th century, and in 1693, Charles II had Luca Giordano decorate them with frescoes giving an impressive barroque appearance.

Giordano is known in Spain as Lucas Jordan thanks to the great amount of work he

▲ *Cenotaph of Philip II, in the Basilica's Main Chapel. On the right, Cenotaph of Charles V in the Basilica's Main Chapel. Leoni.*

Detail of the Cenotaph of Philip II. Leoni. ▶

did, not only here, but in Naples for Spain. Because of his skill and speed, he was assigned great quantities of work and he was deservedly nicknamed "Fa presto" or "the speedy". Giordano painted these ceilings and the one above the Monastery staircase in only 22 months, from September, 1692 to July 1694, when he was 57 years old.

In addition to the large altars-reliquaries painted by Federico Zuccaro, which are situated at the head of the two side aisles (*The Annunciation* and St *Jerome in the Desert*) there are another *forty retables* (thirty-six in the church, and two in the Sotacoro) adorned with canvasses distributed around the various chapels and recesses of the Basilica, which are the work of Juan Fernández de Navarrete "the Dumb", Luis de Carvajal, Diego de Urbina and Alonso Sanchez Coello, all of them Spanish, as well as the Italians Luca Cambiasso, Romulo Cincinnato and Pellegrino Tibaldi.

The decoration of the Basilica is completed by the two large bronze candelabra "el tenebrario" and *"el clavel"*, by Juan Simon de Amberes, around 1571; and the two pulpits by Manuel de Urquiza, commissioned by Ferdinand VII around 1830.

A masterpiece of 16th century Italian sculpture is exhibited in one of the chapels at the foot of the church: the superb *Christ Crucified* in Carrara marble which Benvenuto Cellini sculpted between 1559 and 1562 to be placed above his own tomb in the Florentine Church of the Most Holy Annunciation.

It never occupied this place because the Great Duke of Tuscany persuaded him to sell i

▲ *Lucas Jordán : vault painted with the fresco Exodus of the Israelites.*

Benvenuto Cellini : Christ crucified. *Facade of the Library in the Kings' Courtyard from the Basilica's facade. Below, general* ▲
view of the Kings' Courtyard, with the Basilica's facade.

to him, and he later gave it to Philip II Engraved with the author's name and date on the pedestal, the morbid beauty of this nude sculpture is admirable.

On leaving the Basilica, we once again cross the Patio of Kings, ascending a staircase at the right of vestibule to reach the *Library*, pausing for a moment to contemplate the rigorous beauty of its façade, which looks onto the Patio of the Kings.

The library

THE ORIGINAL plans of the Monastery contemplated the building of a Library as simply another of the many halls and chambers surrounding the Cloister and it did not gain any special or symbolic significance until much later. Given its location, it serves to connect the Convent quarters to the College, (to which it is of common use), and also combines the role of threshold to the central axis of the building: a sort of crossroads of knowledge, faith and power. Not only its location, but also the richness of its decoration, goes to illustrate the importance Philip II attached to the Library within the foundation.

Within the library, the main hall or hall of honour is where books, manufactured with the printing press, are stored. There is another room for printed matter and books that had been banned from circulation. The importance that Philip II, inspired by the outcome of the council of Trent, attached to the Library is in direct proportion to that which he gave to the Seminary and the College as from 1579 onwards. But it was also because of the prestige that a Royal Library lent ot the Spanish Crown, a library which could be considered as the accumulation of knowledge and a Uprecious store" of original codices.

General view of the Library.

Over the centuries, many of the books and manuscripts have been lost – a huge fire destroyed part of the collection in 1671–. Nevertheless, the Library still has over 40,000 editions, including an impressive number of Latin, Greek, Arabic and Hebrew manuscripts.

Apart from its store of 4,000 books and manuscripts which belonged to the Crown and which were kept until then in the Royal Chapel of Granada, the king had several private collections brought to El Escorial. Father Sigüenza and Benito *Arias Montano* Arias Montano were charged with the ordering and classification of the immense collection, which was increased during the reign of Philip III by some 4,000 Arabic manuscripts.

Given the number of windows it boasts – seven of which open onto the Patio of Kings and five onto "la Lonja" – the 55 by 10 meter Library is "bright, full of majesty and light". ❚ shelves are a spectacle in themselves and so t◌ are its frescoes. These last, painted between 1586 and 1593 by Pellegrino Tibaldi in the mannerist style, are clearly influenced by Michelangelo. The complex and extensive iconography which mostly represents or depicts the great wise men of Antiquity, was the brainchild of the chronicler of El Escorial′◌ foundation, Brother Jose de Sigüenza.

The series of frescoes by Tibaldi begins at t◌ entrance to the College with a representation ◌ Philosophy, and at the far side, the south side ◌ Convent end, with a representation of Theolog◌ Between the two extremes, the visitor can contemplate the sciences, or the seven liberal arts, as organized under the medieval dictum ◌

▲ *Detail of the fresco painting in the vault of the Library, by Pellegrino Tibaldi.*

One of the sections of the Library. ▲

the Trivium (Grammar, Rhetoric and Dialectics) and that of the Quadrivium (Arithmethic, Music, Geometry and Astrology). There is an allegoric representation of each one of these arts situated in separate sections of the ceiling with two learned disciples of each science depicted in the semicircular "windows" on either side. Below the ceiling, the friezes are adorned with yet more references to the particular science depided directly above.

The finely elaborated *Doric bookcases* were built by Jose Flecha, Juan Senén and Martín de Gamboa according to designs by Juan de Herrera. The books are placed with the leaves facing out so the paper could "breathe", their gold-tinted edges peeping through the fine metal meshing which "enhances the whole, since from bottom to top, it seems as if painted with gold".

The shelves themselves, mounted on marble, are carved form Indian-coloured wood, the cane shafts and the base and capitals from orange wood. The five brown marble tables that are distributed throughout the hall are from the foundational period, while the two octagonal porphyry ones were made by the marble cutter Bartolomé Zumbigo, around 1660. On all of the aforementioned tables, a large collection of terraqueous and celestial globes, maps and astrolabes, etc., are on display, which suggests the scientific cabinet status which the Library undoubtedly had. Bearing witness to this is the fact that we also have there preserved, an armillary sphere, made by Antonio Santucci around 1582, in accordance with the Polemic system, the earthly and celestial spheres of Jean Blaeu from around 1660 and the stone-magnet that was apparently found during the Monastery foundational excavations.

Other elements of cabinet-work worthy of note include the 18th century *cupboard* which is inlaid with ebony and boxwood and which contains the Library's coin collection. Also of

Building and masonry tools. Model of one of the spires of the towers. ▲

El Greco : Martyrdom of Saint Maurice and the Theban Legion. ▲   31

interest is the barroque portico. Built in 1622, it leads onto the corridors of the Alongside this, we descend the Guesthouse staircase which leads us to the Patio of Kings from which we will begin our tour of the Museums.

The museums

ON COMING down from the Library we return to the Patio of Kings, we leave the building and re-enter it through the main doorway of the *northern façade*, where we had purchased our entrance tickets. This was the doorway that led directly to the Palace kitchens, now converted into ticket offices and cafeteria. Through these, or through the vestibule we enter the *Palace or Carriage Patio*, whose eastern and southern galleries are decorated with two series from battles of the Philip II period, one of the XVII century Flemish school, depicting scenes from the Netherlands campaign, the other depicting scenes from the Battle of Lepanto, by Luca Cambiasso.

It is only possible to appreciate its full size from the main floor as half of the building is taken up by a T-shaped two-storey block which used to lodge the kitchen staff. The rest rooms are located here.

The rooms to the East and North of the Patio of carriages (or the Palace) form the *Palace of the Bourbons*. During the epoch of the Austrias, the norther rooms were taken by the ladies and gentlemen of the Court, and the eastern rooms were used by the King's children.

New museums

The entrance is to be found in the centre of the eastern gallery.

▲ *Models of the cranes used to construct the Monastery.*

In the first room, we find on show the coloured wooden carving of *St. Michael Triumphant over Lucifer,* work of the Charles II court sculptress, Luisa Roldán.

On show in the second room is the splendid painting by Domenico Theotokopuli, *The Martyrdom* of *St. Maurice and the Theban Legion.*

Philip II did not like the El Greco painting he had ordered for an altar in the Basilica (it was later replaced by a work by Romulo Cincinnato) for "decorative" reasons or because its holy

images did not conform to CounterReformation art. Various Flemish tapestries from the Philip II collection are distributed around the two rooms, the famous series of the *Triumph of the Mother of God,* known as the *Paños de Oro,* being among the most outstanding.

The Monastery Architecture Museum

By means of the staircase behind the El Greco painting we descend to these rooms, opened in

On the left, Paolo Cagliari, from Verona: the Annunciation, and on the right, Juan Fernández de Navarrete, the Mute: the slitting ▲
of Santiago's throat.

1963 and lately enhanced as a result of the exhibitions held there in 1986, which house a didactic collection containing plans, models etc., that are fundamentally self-explanatory.

Museum of art

The Museum of Art is located in the halls below the House of the *King*, that is the so-called Summer *Palace*, which were renovated in 1963 to exhibit those paintings amassed in the Monastery over the centuries that were not transferred to the Prado Museum in the 19th and 20th centuries Below we will describe the present layout, given that, as is logical, variations may be introduced.

Along with paintings from the 16th century Venetian school, the first room brings together other fine examules such as the magnificent St *Michael* by Luca Cambiasso.

The Venetian works worth noting are: St Margaret by Tiziano; *The Maydalen* by Tintoretto; and *The Eternal Father* by Paolo Veronese, whose studio was responsible for *The Descent,* a reduced version of which, painted by his son, Carlo Veronese, is also exhibited in this room.

The second room is dedicated to Flemish art from the 16th and 17th centuries.

From the 16th century, there are two major works: *The Seven Liberal Arts* Martin de Vos and *The Judgement* of *Solomon* by Pieter Aertsen, the latter dated 1562. From the 17th century, some fine examples are *The Supper* of *Emaus* by Rubens; Van Dyk's a *Virgin* and *Hight to Egypt* and *The Martvrdon of St. Justine,* painted by Giordiano in the style of Rubens.

The third room is dedicated in its entirety to the Flemish painter Miguel Coxcie, one of Philip II's favourite painters, whose work is profoundly influenced by Italian painting, as a result of his study of the work of Raphael and Leonardo. Worthy of note are the *Christ under the burden of the Cross, David and Goliath* and the *St. Philip Triptych,* painted in honour of the King's Patron Saint.

The three interior rooms, (the fourth, fifth, an' sixth) whose windows look onto the Patio of Masks, display Italian, Spanish and Dutch paintings mainly from the 17th century. Worth noting are *The* Journey of Jacob by Andrea di Leoni and the Portrait of Innocent X by Pietro Martire Neri in the fourth room; The Two *Still Lifes* by Juan van de Hamen and two *Floreros* by Daniel Seghers in the fifth: and in the sixth. *Lot Intoxicated by his daughters* by Guercino.

The long seventh room, the former Gallery of Walks of the summer Palace, with excellent views of the gardens an Madrid, houses some of the most famous canvasses conserved in the Monastery which are also strongly linked to the history of its foundation, such as the ones originally chosen for the Basilica´s main altar and later discarded.

These are *The Annunciation* by Veronese, *The Adoration* of *the Shepherds* by Tintoretto and *the Nativity* and *The Epiphany* by Federico Zuccaro.

Facing, the great works of the painter Juan Fernandez de Navarrete, the Dumb are of interest, such as *The Beheading of St. James* and *St. Jerome Repentant.* Between these two paintings, you can find the excellent copy by Coxcie of *The Descent,* the original of which (previously in El Escorial and now in the Prado Museum) was painted by the 15th century Flemish artist, Van der Weyden, the author of *The Calvary* which is hung on the front *wall* of the same.room. *The Calling of St. Peter and St. Andrew* by the Italian Federico Barocci is on the opposite wall.

The eighth room is dedicated to 17th century Spanish painting. You can admire here works by Jose de Ribera, the "Españoleto", the leading figure of the 17th century Neopolitan

Roger Van der Weyden: The Calvary. ▶

school, although he was born in Valencia: *Apparition of the Child to St Anthony*, a St Jerome Repentant, as well as some copies; *The Presentation of the Virgin in the Temple*.

The ninth room - originally Philip II's summer bedroom leading onto the gallery of the "underground church" which he used as private chapel, and which is now the Pantheon of the Kings is dedicated to Luca Giordano and some 17th century Spanish painters. Two paintings of the *Virgin with Child* by Alonso Cano are worth noting here.

A corridor from the last room in the Museum of Art leads out to the *Patio of Masks*.

Patio of Masks

THIS PATIO, which is overshadowed by the enormous façade of the Church, owes its name to the two fountains in its eastern wall; the rest of the patio is surrounded by porticos formed by semi-circled arches on Tuscan columns, which is typical of the country house style of this royal residence. In addition to the so obviously inspired Italian design of this patio, a touch of Flemish influence can be noted from the roofs and the curious chimney tops, which were the only part of this building left untouched by the terrible fire of 1671, the *House of the King*, which is built around the patio on two floors, with the summer rooms, as we have already seen, on the ground floor and the winter rooms on the main one, as we are about to see.

The House of the King

THE HOUSE of the King is symbolically located in the central axis of the building, and is joined

▲ *The Courtyard of Heads.*

General view of the Gallery of Battles. Fresco paintings by Granello, Castello, Cambiasso and Tavarone. ▶

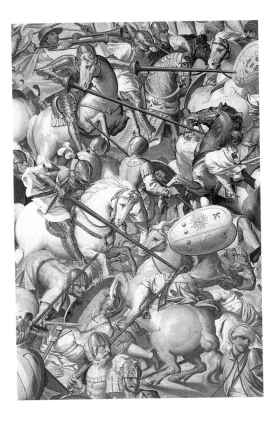

closely to the sanctuary in such a fashion that the figure of the King appears as if protected by Divine Grace and as defender of the Faith; mediator between the sacred and the profane (Monastery and Palace), but at the same time separated from mere mortals by these rooms where "no-one without license can enter, like an eagle in its eyrie". The House of the King is, despite its modest size and appearance, the centre of the entire Monastery, since from here, the Sacred Monarch had access to all parts of the Monastery.

As all the palaces of the Spanish Monarchs of that time, this one at El Escorial was divided into two similarly laid-out chambers for both the *King* and the Queen. They were situated in such a fashion that they could see through the adjoining private chapel and from their respective bedrooms the high altar of the

church. "Luckily the monarchs were lodged within and yet outside the main chapel, the design of which would not have been more dignified or more great". The Queen's chamber is attributed the highest honour by being located on the side of the Evangel (on the left, if one looks towards the altar); as the King became a widower for the fourth and last time in 1580, the Queen's chamber was used by her daughter, Isabel Clara Eugenia, which is why i is named the *Chamber of the Infanta*. Ascending from the Patio of Masks by means of the Queen's staircase one can enter the Queen's Chamber, or that of the Infanta, but one can also come out onto the last hall of the "Public Palace", which is adjoined to The House of the King: The Gallery of Battles is covered in frescoes depicting war scenes (hence de name) painted by Fabrizio Castello, Orazio Cambiass

▲ *On the left, detail of the fresco Battle of Higueruela in the Gallery of Battles and on the right, general view of the Portrait Room.*

and Lazzaro Tavarone. These "long works", as they are known, were typical of that period and were used for covered walks as well as for solemn receptions.

Here, Philip II wanted to demonstrate the connection between is campaigns for European hegemony and the bellicose attitude of the Spanish Christian monarchs of the Middle Ages. The *Battle of Higueruela*, John II of Castile's victory over the natives of Granada in 431, painted on the long wall facing the windows (it is a copy of a long 15th century sketch found in the Alcázar of Segovia) is set off against several scenes depicted on the front walls and the walls between the balconies. These are of the *Battle of San Quentin* from the Portuguese campaign, and the clashes with the English in the Azores, which all took place during Philip II's reign.

Entering from the Queen's or Infanta's Chamber one reaches the *Ante-chamber*, and from this to the Chamber or bedroom of the female infant. The chancel of the church can be seen from this chamber and the *Gardens of the Queen* from the windows.

The portrait of *Isabel Clara Eugenia* by Bartolomé González hangs next to her sister's, *Catalina Micaela* from the Sánchez Coello school. The small *hand organ* is from the 16th century *16th* century, and has Philip II's coat-of-arms on its face.

You return to the Ante-Chamber by going around the corridors above the Patio of Masks which join the King's chamber with the Queen's. This *Ante-Chamber* is decorated with various paintings by Juan Correa de Vivar and from the Bassano studio. Philip II's *hand chair is* also found in this chamber.

The chair, which was used by the gout-ridden King in the last years of his life, has a curious system for dismantling the back. The structure allowed for a canopy to be placed on top and the sides closed off. You then come to the *King's* Quarters. The sequence of distribution and use of the rooms were governed in the Spanish royal palaces by Burgundian etiquette, imposed by Charles V, which reinforced the "sacred" identity of the Monarch: each room has a successively more restricted entrance, depending on the visitor's rank.

The Talavera tiled frieze covering the lower part of the walls is original. In general, the furnishing of these rooms reflects what is known today as 16th century decoration.

From the Ante-Chamber, you reach the *Hall of Portraits,* which owes its name to the royal portraits of the House of Austria exhibited there. They are the works of Pantoja de la Cruz, Sanchez Coello, Antonio Moro and Juan Carreño.

This room was used for common audiences with the King. The Chinese foldable chairs from the Ming era (second half of the 16th century) were used by the King to rest his gouty leg. Among the most noteworthy of the portraits is the Antonio Moro portrait of *Philip II* at the age of 35, believed to be dressed in the armour of the *Battle of San Quentin.*

From the Hall of portraits along the Gallery of Walks to the King's Chamber, you pass through two wooden inlaid doors "of the best and best carved to come to us from Germany, expertly designed", sent as a gift by the Emperor Maximilian II to Philip II in 1567.

The Gallery of Walks, inside the King's Chamber, was a typical feature of 16th century European palaces which served for indoor strolls when the weather was bad.

The description of Father Sigüenza has, more or less, been followed, as regards hanging

Chinese foldable chair used by Philip II. Door of German marquetry in the Strolling Gallery.

Antonio Moro : Philip II.

canvasses which depict military actions from the epoch of Philip II (there were Flemish landscapes here before), and map engravings due to the famous XVI century geographer Abraham Ortelius. The *meridians*, on the floor of this room and the following, are the work of the Jesuit father Juan Wedlingen (1755).The two interior rooms parallel to this gallery looking out onto the Patio of Masks , parallel to this gallery and which can be seen from the doors, are decorated with paintings from the 16th and 17th centuries, among which worthy of note are: *The Moneychanger and his wife* by Marinus van Reymerswaele, and *The Virgin with the Child* by Quentin Metsys.

In the *King's Chamber* or *the Ante-Chamber*, there is a complete series of 17th century anonymous paintings of Philip II's royal residences around Madrid . This series demonstrates the taste for architecture and passion for building of the Sovereign, even while he was still Prince. His greatest architectural achievement is undoubtedly the El Escorial Monastery, of which some engravings by Pedro Perret, based on designs by Juan de Herrera, are also exhibited.

This series is fundamental for an understanding of the building. These engraving were here in Philip II's time in addition to "still life paintings of many things found in our New World: some of the many different species of fowl... others of a great variety of large and small animals... and others of a thousand insects", a product of the great scientific work o Philip II's proto-doctor, Francisco Hernández.

By crossing a corridor that encircles the *King's staircase,* you reach *Philip II's bedchamber* where he died on September l3th, 1598:

"..in the same house and temple of San Lorenzo that he himself had built, ...

▲ *King's Chamber.*

almost above his own tomb, at five o'clock in the morning, when the dawn was breaking in the East ... the seminary children were singing the dawn mass, the last mass they gave for his health, and the first for his salvation".

The position of his bed, which had been inspired by his father's bed in Yuste, allowed the King to see, from his bedside, the countryside through the two balconies and, on the other side, his chapel and the Basilica's high altar. On the table in the study, there is a "watchtower" – the work of Philip II's clockmaker, the German, Hans of Evalo.

Signed in 1583, it is a typical mannerist piece. The Monarch used only the light of his little oil lamp when he wrote at night. The King's Bedchamber was decorated in its day among other things with *The Table of the Mortal Sins* by Bosch, now in the Prado Museum. Among the paintings exhibited today in the

King's Chamber, with the study and the bedroom. At the back, the oratory. Below, "Clock of custody", by Hans de Evalo, 1583. ▲

bedchamber are the *Sacra conversazione* by Benvenuto Tisi, il Garofolo; a *Pietà* by Gerard David and *The Portrait of Philip II* as an old man by Pantoja de la Cruz. The ebony, silver and bronze retable is a Roman piece by Antonio Gentili following the design of Giuliano della Porta, and was a gift from the Great Duchess of Tuscany to the King in 1586. The rest of the paintings, all on pious themes, are Flemish and Italian from the early 1 6th century.

There are several precious objects worthy of note in the cupboard, two *medieval chests or boxes*: one made of bone from the X century, and the other from the Limoges workshop dating from the XII century; from the XVI century we have the *portapaz plateresco* ('silvery peace plate') in the form of a pavilion by the famous goldsmith Luis del Castillo; and from the end of the same century two *agate paintings* said to be by Annibale Carracci.

The austerity of these chambers is quite surprising given the royal pomp and splendou of the Modern Age and the fact that Philip II, King of Spain and the New World, was the most important European Monarch of the century. Nonetheless, one must take into account that this was the "Royal Chamber" of the Monastery's founder inside the building itself in which Philip II, following the medieva tradition, used to live and cultivate his religious and filial piousness.

▲ *King's oratory, seen from the Basilica's presbytery.*

Leaving these rooms, you go down a corridor and, descending, we arrive at the vestibule between the *Basilica* and the *Ante-Sacristy*, from which we continue descending until we get to the *Pantheons*

The Pantheons

ONE OF El Escorial's main functions is the burial place for the Spanish Monarchs. Nevertheless, this did not materialize until after the founder's death, who had said, according to biographical notes, that he had built a dwelling place for God; and that his son, if he so wished, could do so for his bones, and

then the bones of his parents. The two Pantheons reflect two distinct styles and centuries: the barroque style of the 17th century for the *Kings* and *Queens*, and the eclectic 19th century for the Infantes or their children.

The Pantheons are reached by a stairway which stems from the church to the Sacristy. The left branch leads to the Pantheons of the Kings and the right to the Infantes'.

The *Pantheons of the Kings* is a dome-covered circular chamber whose circumference is divided into eight sections. Juan de Herrera conceived and built it in granite, but when Philip III decided to convert it into a Pantheon, he had the overseer of the royal constructions, Giovanni Battista

Access door to the Kings' Mausoleum. On the right, Altar of the Kings' Mausoleum. ▲

On the following double page, general view of the Kings' Mausoleum. ▶

Crescenzi, surface it in marble and bronze, according to a project by Juan Gómez de Mora, begun in 1617. The work was prolonged because of difficulties that arose throughout almost all of Philip IV's reign, and was not completed until 1654.

Crescenzi, a Roman, directed the work done in bronze, carried out by Italian, in particular, Genovese artesans. The marble work was led by Pedro de Lizargárate and Bartolomé Zumbigo, the Elder. It was during Philip IV's reign that the solution to the technical problems was found (a spring had appeared when the floor was lowered), along with the addition of grotesques to the dome, the new floor design and all the surfacing of the stairway and its doors, the gilding of the bronzes and the inclusion of some more. The richness of the marble (the blue-tint from Toledo and the red from Tortosa) and the bronze, the Corinthian pomp and the exuberant barroque of the grotesques make this chamber a fine example of early Italian barroque, giving it a more international than Spanish air. Presiding over the altar is a *Christ Crucified* by Domenico Guidi, a less well-known artist, but more fortunate that Gian Lorenzo Bernini and Pietro Tacca who had previously produced other crucifixes for the same altar, but which are now kept in the College chapel and in the Sacristy vestry respectively.

The remains (after having previously laid for years in an adjoining temporary vault, the "Pudridero") of the monarchs and their wives lie in the urns, that is, only the wives who had borne their husbands children; the kings on the right and the queens on the left, placed in chronological order from Charles I to Alphonse XIII, which spans a period of four centuries of the Spanish Monarchy; the only bodies absent are those of Philip V and his son Philip VI, as well as their respective wives, given that they wished to be buried in their respective foundations of La

▲ *Tomb of Don Juan of Austria, in the fifth chamber of the Mausoleum of Princes and Princesses. Below, detail of the vault of the Chapterhouses.*

Granja de San Ildefonso and the Salesas Reales Monastery in Madrid.

The *Pantheon of the Infantes* was built on the orders of Isabella II, based on a project by José Segundo de Lema, and was completed in 1888. Each of the nine chambers, located beneath the Sacristy and the Chapter Houses, are presided over by an altar and surfaced in marble. The sculptures and adornments were produced in Carrara by Jacobo Baratta di Leopoldo modelled on work by Ponciano Ponzano. The style of this Pantheon, inspired in historical sources gives rise to some new and truly funereal architectural forms. The cold aspect, the historic interest and the 19th century spirit pervading the Pantheon all add to its richness and attraction.

The most outstanding of the nine rooms are: first chamber: neoclasic altar with a Descend of Carlo Veronese, tombs of María Josefa de Borbón, by G. Velázquez, of the mother in law of Isabel II, Luisa Carlota de Borbón, the Dukes of Monpensier, and that of their daughters by Aimé Millet. The *fifth chamber*, contains the sepulchre of D. Juan de Austria, which is the work of Giuseppe Galeotti following the design of Ponzano. The *sixth chamber* is occupied by a mausoleum of the Kings' children who died before reaching puberty, which resembles a sort

Sixth Chamber of the Mausoleum of Princes and Princesses. ▲

of twenty-sided tart in white marble. On the altar, there is a fine painting, The Virgin of the Veil, by Lavinia Fontana (1590). The *ninth chamber* has the most historical interest as it contains sixteen tombs pertaining to the House of Austria.

At the far end of the Pantheon of the Infantes, you find two arched cellars called the "silversmiths' workshops" from which a stairway leads up to the *Chapter Houses*.

The Chapter Houses

THESE RATHER impressive and large Chapter Houses surrounded by a wooden bench were designed for the assemblies of the one hundred

monks that lived in the Monastery. Two ro are separated by a central entrance hallwa *Vicarial* and the *Prioral,* whose names come from the vicar or prior who presided over them. The last square room beneath the to is the lower *Priory Cell.* These Chapter Hou the Priory Cell and the entrance hallway fo magnificent row of four rooms, whose vau ceilings are painted with frescoes of grotes motifs by Fabrizio Castello and Nicola Granello. Most of the canvasses that used t hang on the walls are now part of the Prad Museum collection however, the remaining works are also fine examples of art.

Pride of place in the *Vicarial* Room is Tiziano's St Jerome Repentant. Alongside a the two *flower paintings* by Mario Nuzzi, cal

▲ *Diego Velázquez:* Joseph's Coat.

"dei fiori", and the two eremite saints, St *Paul* and *St Jerome* by José de Ribera, who also painted the three magnificent canvasses hanging on the long wall facing the windows: St *Francis Receiving the Stigmata, Jacob with his Flock* and *a Pietà*. One of the Spanish masters's works is also exhibited here: Diego Velázquez's *The Tunic of Joseph*, painted during his first stay in Rome. Some of El Greco's most celebrated works hang between the windows. They are *The Adoration of the Name of Jesus* which is an allegory of the painting. The Holy Alliance of Philip II, the Pope and Venice against the Turks in 1571.

The *Prioral Room* is mainly decorated with Venetian art: Tiziano's *The Prayer in the Garden*, which presides the altar, as well as his *The Rest on the Flight to Egypt* and *The Last Supper* which was, unfortunately, cut down to size to fit on the on the Monastery refectory wall; Tintoretto's *Esther before Asuero* and *Christ and Magdalene in the Pharisee's house* Veronese's *The Descent of Christ to Limbo* and Moretto da Brescia's The *Eritrean Prophetress* and *The Prophet Isaias*.

The Gospel lecterns, the work of Juan Simon de Amberes in 1571, are exhibited in the centre of the room. In the *Priory Cell*, there is

▲ *Tiziano :* The Last Supper. *Below, José de Ribera :* Saint Francis of Assisi.

still a collection of Hyeronimus Bosch's, known in Spain as "El Bosco", board paintings, which include *The* Calvary Way, *The Haycart* and *The Crown of Thorns.* Above the altar, you can see the *portable retable of Emperor Charles V*, which is a splendid example of enamelled and wooden gold-plated silver put together by different workshops. The relief work and the apostles are more Italianized and the three apexes are of a later and more international mannerist style.

The Main Cloister

THE MAIN Cloister galleries around the Patio of the Evangelists are decorated with fifty-four frescoes depicting the *Story of* the *Redemption* from the birth of the Virgin until the Last Judgement. They go in order from the

Procession Door, which joins the Cloister with the church. This series is painted by Pellegrino Tibaldi and his studio. The "stations" in the corners are by Luis de Carvajal, Cincinnato, Tibaldi and Miguel Barroso.

The main staircase

THE MAIN staircase is found in the centre of the western gallery of the Cloister. This "impressive and beautiful" staircase was not based on Juan Bautista de Toledo designs, but was apparently the work of Gian Battista Castello, known as the Bergamasco. Added to its attractive architectural design is the lavishness of the fresco ceiling painted in 1692 by Luca Giordano: *The Glory of the Spanish Monarchy.* Charles II, depicted in the centre of

▲ *Main lower Cloister Gallery.*

Lucas Jordán : The Glory of Spanish Monarchy. ▶

the western wall, is showing this apotheosis to his mother, Mariana of Austria and to his wife Mariana of Neoburg.

Once one has seen the staircase, it is worthwhile going for a stroll around the galleries and contemplating the paintings and the Evangelist templete. There are a few more places of interest around the Cloister, like the *Old Church* and the *Sacristy*, but they are closed to the public.

The patio of the Evangelists

THIS IS one of the most interesting arcas in the building from an architectural point of view as much for the gallery façades of the Cloister, based on a Juan Bautista de Toledo design modified by Juan de Herrera, as for the Temple (the work of Herrera) and which gives the patio its name.

The patio garden, laid out in a typically cloistered style – in the shape of a cross – is encircled by a Doric building in allusion not only to the fountain of Grace and spiritual life (the Four Gospels), but also to the Garden of Eden with the four rivers which irrigate the four corners of the world: this Temple of the Evangelists was designed in 1586 by Juan de Herrera; the sculptures are by Juan Bautista Monegro.

The Old Church was on loan, that is to say, it served as a temporary worship place for the monks form 1571 until the Basilica was completed in 1586. The three very impressive marble retables are conserved in their original state. On the biggest retable, you can see one of Tiziano's masterpieces: the magnificent *Martyrdom of St. Lawrence*. There are no words to describe the courage of this work; a similar one, albeit a little earlier, exists in the Jesuit Church in Venice.

Despite being closed to the public, this vast rectangular hall is worth mentioning for several reasons. Its ceiling is painted with grotesques by Granello and Castello. The paintings on its wall are some of the best in the Monastery, and you can still find an odd treasure or two, such as Tiziano's *Christ Crucified*, a *St Peter freed by an angel* by Ribera and several canvasses by Jordán. The finest example is the masterpiece painted by the head of the Madrid school after Velazquez's death, Claudio Coello's *The Adoration of the Holy Ghost by Charles II*, in which baroque ingenuity gives imaginary depth to the sacristy scene and depicts the ceremony just as it was celebrated in this very room in October, 1684 – a true snapshot of the Spanish Court. This painting has an anecdotal tale to tell as it also serves as a screen or veil to conceal the chamber of the Holy Ghost to reveal it only on special occasions. And so, the painting actually descends, sliding down the railings until it disappears from view

Claudio Coello : detail of Charles II's adoration of the Holy Form.

Shrine by Juan de Herrera, with sculptures by Juan Bautista Monegro, in the Courtyard of Evangelists.

completely, and we are left with the wonderful sight of the *Crucifix* by Pietro Tacca, and the Neo-gothic tabernacle in substitution of the Baroque one which disappeared during the Napoleonic invasion. The work on the retable and the vestry was based on a José del Olmo design. From the Cloister we go out onto the Basilica Porch, from which we can enter the latter (p. 20), or once again going outside in order to enter through the northern façade, we arrive at Palace or Carriage Patio from where we can gain access to the Palace of the Bourbons.

The Palace of the Bourbons

BY PREVIOUS appointment, you can go on a guided tour of the Palace on Friday afternoons and Saturdays. An appointment may be made by phoning 91-890 59 02/5.

The Bourbon quarters take up the eastern and northern sides of the Carriage or Palace Patio. During the epoch of the Austrias, the internal bays looking out onto the Patio consisted of two enormous galleries; of the two external bays, the eastern one was occupied by the Royal Family, while the northern one was given over to rooms for the main courtiers. Charles III had all these spaces adapted to better accommodate the Royal Family, especially that of the Prince of Asturias, because he lived, as did his predecessors, in the "handle of the grille", that was also decorated according to Bourbon taste, until the reign of Alfonso XIII. Nevertheless, when Charles IV assumed the throne he did not want to occupy the secular King's Chamber, but to continue in the rooms to which he was accustomed, and in order to give them a more dignified entrance, he had Villanova construct a decorative staircase, and completely modify the northern

façade of the Monastery. Given the coherence in its decoration, the richness of the tapestries from the Royal Factory at Santa Barbara in Madrid, and the relatively good preservation its layout, it is the most characteristic of all the Spanish Bourbon palaces.

The access to the Palace is via a staircase built by the architect Juan de Villanueva in 179 From the higher landing, three passageways lead to the royal chambers corresponding to three royal personages. We will follow that which leads the way to the *King's room*.

The three small rooms on the furthest west on the northern side were the *workshops of Charles IV*. In these rooms several paintings by Mariano Salvador Maella of religious themes ar worthy of note, as are three bisque porcelain pieces from the Royal Factory at Naples, with portraits of the Royal Family. Next we have the China Room, so-called because of the Neo-classical style sideboard, where there is an English porcelain crockery set from the Copelar factory on display, a gift from the British King George V to Alfonso XIII and Doña Victoria Eugenia on the occasion of their wedding.

Next we have the rooms decorated with tapestries from the Royal Factory at Santa Bárbara on models, or "cartoons", painted by the artists that are indicated, and made to measure for the walls of this Palace, and in the majority of cases for El Pardo. The tapestries thus completely cover the walls in order to protect the royal personages from the cold, given that the El Escorial "workday" took place in autumn, and that of the El Pardo in winter. Perhaps this desire to offer cosy and warm surroundings goes to explain the relatively small dimensions of the rooms. Originally, the cartoons for each room were given to one artist with a unifying theme, which granted the decoration a stylistic and plot coherence that we have lost today, to a large extent due to the

Anteroom of Ambassadors.

many changes of place from the end of the XVIII century and the beginning of the XIX century, which in the majority of cases must be respected.

The Gala Dining Room, and old piece of tricks, it has tapestries after cartoons by Goya, Bayeu and Castillo. The following piece serves as a *hall* from the Villanueva staircase: Anglois, Antonio González Velázquez and Calleja imitating Teniers and Wouwerman compositions. The Goya and Bayeu ante-room. *The Ambassadors' Salon*, Bayeu. The piece from the King's chapel, on whose altar there is a Holy Family by Luca Giordano, is to be found in the right-angle of the Palace Patio: up to here all the line of rooms whose balconies to the Patio are facing South have been passed through, and one continues along the façade that looks towards the West.

The first four rooms belong to the Infantas' Quarters, and the last two to the Queen's Chamber. The first is the Infantas' Old Playroom, known today as the Telemachus because of the "adventures of the young hero", depicted on the tapestries woven in Brussels by Leyniers. From here on all the tapestries are once again from the Royal Factory at Madrid. The following piece is the Dormitory, with tapestries after cartoons by Bayeu and Aguirre. *Pieces of the Nannies*, known as the Pompeian Salon, by Agustín and Juan Navarro. *The Entrance piece* by Goya, Castillo and Bayeu. *The Queen's Chamber Attendants Salon*, with hunting scenes by Goya, Castillo and Aguirre. From here, we can see the last line of rooms, the *Entrance Piece to the Queen's Chamber*, which leads directly to the Gallery of Battles and is decorated with tapestries after compositions of Teniers.

All the following rooms, look out onto the eastern façade, and from the fine wood pieces, to the north. *The Queen's Court Room*, with

Bedroom, called the King's, in the Bourbon Palace.

scenes from Bayeu, Goya and Castillo, among others; magnificent consoles carved in Charles IV period, and in the centre, an English piano from the beginning of the XIX century, by Thomas Tomkinson. From this piece, we go to the Chapel, with candelabras and gold gilded silver accessories, from the Mártinez Royal Factory at Madrid. *Daily Dining Room*, an old *dresser piece*, with tapestries after cartoons by Goya, Aguirre and Castillo. *Dormitory* – today called the King's Bedroom –, with a magnificent French made bed, from the transition period between Neo-classical and Imperial, which belonged to Charles IV. The *Washroom*, with scenes from Castillo and Aguirre, among others, Fernandine furniture and a curious structure which receives the water closet with a Neo-classical mural decoration.

Dormitory – nowadays called the Queen's Bedroom –, with tapestries of sights of Madrid by Aguirre. *The Seamstress' Piece*, which maintains in their original location the tapestries with Pompeian motifs by Castillo, woven to decorate this "oval piece" corresponding to the room of the then Princess of Asturias, María Luisa de Parma. The *Audience Salon,* with scenes from Goya, Bayeu and Castillo, is furnished with a strange Neo-gothic decorative ensemble from the epoch of Fernando VII, made by Angel Maeso the cabinet maker in 1832.

Next are the so-called *rooms of fine wood*, representative of the culmination of the high international standards reached in inlaywork and decorative arts of Charles IV style. Decorative work on these four rooms – the office, what was called the ante-chamber of the Prie Dieu, private chapel and water closet – contained marbles of Indian wood inlay, and took from 1793 to 1831 to complete. The ornamental motifs are inspired in the classicist style, in Pompeian forms and in those of Robert Adam, among other European genuises of the

Monks' Garden from the Convalescent Gallery or "Sun Corridors". ▲

late 18th century. Diverse tendencies are united here in rich and elaborate harmony.

The gardens

ONCE YOU have finished your visit to the building, it is worthwhile enjoying the gardens, and other works on outside. Walking along the main façade, and descending the "la Lonja" stairs, we come across the gallery which joins the Monastery and the "Compaña". Below the latter, a door leads onto the Patio of the Chemist, and from there, onto the *Gallery of Convalescents* by Juan Bautista de Toledo.

"This beautiful example of architecture and brickwork which forms two separated façades in these gardens owes its grace to the unmatching archways." As the name sugges these "sun passageways" were meant for convalescing monks, while at the same time, they served to conceal the retaining wall and link the garden and "la Lonja".

The Friar's Garden

The Friar's Garden is situated in the area betw the walls which were built to support the Monastery; the two parallel staircases lead to garden, which is graced with a beautiful *pond* Francisco de Mora. When returning to leave th garden, it is worthwhile going to the extreme the railing over the pond in order to see from there the Monastery's southern façade. Follow this pathway, we arrive at the Upper House.

▲ *King's private garden and Prior's Tower.*

External view of the "Upper Little House" or Little House of the Prince and its gardens, to the south-west of the Monastery.

The Upper House of the House of the Infante

The so-called House of the Infante or Upper House, was built by Juan de Villanueva between 1771 and 1773 for the Infante Don Gabriel, the son of Charles III. Its noble ionic architecture includes an Italian-styled terraced garden which offers one of the best views of the Monastery. It is open to the public during Holy Week and the summer months, except Mondays.

The ground plan of this pleasant leisure casino, built around a two-storey high central chamber was originally designed for chamber concerts, and in the last analysis, from Palladian models. Typical of Villanueva is the entrance span with columns framed by sections.

Finally, a stroll coming down from the northern façade of the Monastery, through a fenced-off park which leads us to the Lower House.

The Lower House or the House of the Prince

The House of the Prince or Lower House, was built around the same time as the House of the Infante for Don Gabriel's elder brother, the future Charles IV, by Juan de Villanueva. It was later enlarged between 1781 and 1784 by the same architect. As well as being bigger, this House has an advantage over the Infante's in that its interior decoration is in a much better condition.

The architectural design of the House of the Prince (also seen in the House of the Infante, but to a lesser degree) perfectly combines the main building with the smaller ones and its formal garden, which was also designed by Villanueva, but later ruined due to the planting of pine trees in the late 19th and early 20th centuries. Extensions were made to the large drawing room and the oval room, in 1781, giving the ground plan a T-shape, and to the upper part of

the west garden with the addition of the pond. On the ground floor, the "Pompeian" painted ceilings are by Manuel Pérez, Felipe López, Jua Duque and Vicente Gómez. Most of the paintings representing religious, allegorical or mythological scenes are by the Neapolitans, Lu Giordano and Corrado Giaquinto. The piece o furniture worthy of note is the large drawing room table, with a magnificent board of hard stones from the Buen Retiro Royal Laboratory Corynthian columns, from the Charles IV peri

From the garden of this house, the Basilica dome can be seen above the Park tree tops. It i 92 metres high, 20 higher than the bell towers and 47 higher than the towers. Since enough h been said about the Monastery's "qualities", a since it is customary to inform people about certain of the Monastery's "quantities", somed who did do a count calculated that the whole building had 296 exterior windows, with a tot number of 2,600; 1,200 doors, 86 staircases, 88 fountains, 16 patios, 15 cloisters and 9 towers, within an area of 207 by 161 square meters.

Vault of the central room of the Little House of the Prince.

Main facade and porch of the "Lower Little House" or Little House of the Prince.

Bibliography

HERRERA, Juan de: *Sumario y breve declaración de los diseños y estampas de la fábrica de San Lorenzo el Real del Escorial*, Madrid, 1589 (facsimile editions, 1954 y 1978).

SIGÜENZA, José de: *Fundación del Monasterio de El Escorial.* –Books 3 and 4 of *Historia de la Orden de San Jerónimo* (Madrid, 1605)–, Ed. Turner, Madrid, 1986.

SANTOS, Francisco de los: *Descripción del Real Monasterio de San Lorenzo del Escorial, única maravilla del mundo*, Madrid, 1657.

XIMÉNEZ, Andrés: *Descripción del Real Monasterio de San Lorenzo del Escorial: Su magnífico templo, panteón y Palacio*, Madrid, 1764.

BERMEJO, Damián: *Descripción artística del Real Monasterio de San Lorenzo del Escorial y sus preciosidades después de la invasión de los franceses*, Madrid, 1820.

LLAGUNO y AMIROLA, Eugenio: *Noticias de los arquitectos y arquitectura desde su restauración, por don Eugenio Llaguno y Amirola, ilustradas y acrecentadas con notas, adiciones y documentos por don Juan Agustín Ceán Bermúdez*, 4 volumes, Madrid, 1829.

QUEVEDO, José de: *Historia del Real Monasterio de San Lorenzo*, Madrid, 1849.

ROTONDO, Antonio: *Historia descriptiva, artística y pintoresca del Real Monasterio de San Lorenzo, vulgarmente llamado de El Escorial*, Madrid, 1863.

RUIZ DE ARCAUTE, Agustín: *Juan de Herrera, arquitecto de Felipe II*, Madrid, 1936.

HENERMANN, Theodor: "El Escorial en la crítica estético-literaria del extranjero, esbozo de una historia de su fama", in *El Escorial: Revista de cultura y letras*, 1943, pp. 319-341.

LÓPEZ SERRANO, Matilde: *Trazas de Juan de Herrera y sus seguidores para el Monasterio de El Escorial*, Madrid, 1944.

LORENTE JUNQUERA, Manuel: "La galería de convalecientes, obra de Juan de Herrera", *Archivo Español de Arte*, 17, num. 63, 1944, pp. 137-147.

PORTABALES, Amancio: *Los verdaderos artífices El Escorial y el estilo indebidamente llamado herreriano*, Madrid, 1945.

ZUAZO UGALDE, Secundino: *Los orígenes arquitectónicos del Real Monasterio de San Lorenzo del Escorial*, Madrid, 1948.

PORTABALES PICHEL, Amancio: *Maestros mayores, arquitectos y aparejadores de El Escorial*, Madrid, 1952.

ÁLVAREZ TURIENZO, Saturnino: *El Escorial en letras españolas*, Madrid, 1963.

AA.VV.: *Monasterio de San Lorenzo el Real de El Escorial*. Patrimonio Nacional. El Escorial, 1964, 2 volumes.

CHUECA GOITIA, Fernando: *Casas Reales en Monasterios y Conventos españoles*, Madrid, R.A.H., 1966, Madrid, Xarait, 1982.

TAYLOR, René: "Architecture and magic: Considerations on the idea of the Escorial", *Ensays in the history of architecture in honor of Rudolf Wittkower*, Phaidon, Londres, 1967 (Spanish edition with revised and extended text: Ediciones Siruela, S.A., Madrid, 1992).

KUBLER, George: *Building the Escorial*, Princeton, 1982. Spanish ed., Alianza Editorial, Madrid,

OSTEN SACKEN, Cornelia Von der: *El Escorial estudio iconológico*, Madrid, Xarait, 1984.

RIVERA BLANCO, Javier: *Juan Bautista de Toledo Felipe II. La implantación del clasicismo en Esp* Universidad de Valladolid, 1984.